My Body

by Lola M. Schaefer

Table of Contents

I can run fast and jump high. I can ride my bike and race with my friends. I can do these things because I take care of my body.

What Does My Body Need?

My body needs sleep. I need
ten hours of sleep each night.
Sleep helps my body grow strong.

Children need two to six more hours of sleep
than adults.

My body should have clean teeth. I brush and floss my teeth after every meal. This keeps my teeth clean and white. Brushing helps fight cavities, too.

My body should be clean. I wash
my body every day with soap and water.
Washing with soap helps keep
my body clean. Washing helps take away
old skin cells and germs.

My body needs food. I eat good food every day. Fruits, vegetables, and meat make me strong. Rice, noodles, and bread are good for me, too.

fruits and vegetables

meat and fish

cereal and grains

dairy

My body needs exercise. Exercise keeps my body fit. It makes me strong, too. I need to exercise every day.

My body needs water. I always drink water when I exercise. When my body works hard, it needs a lot of water.

How Do I Keep My Body Safe?

I keep my body safe in many ways.
I keep my skin safe from the sun
with sunscreen.

A helmet keeps my head safe. Knee pads
keep my knees safe. They keep my body
safe from cuts and scrapes.

How else can I keep
my body safe?

How Do I Keep My Body Well?

I try to keep germs out of my body.
Germs can make my body sick.
I keep my hands out of my mouth
and away from my eyes. I wash
my hands often.

Sometimes germs get inside my body and make me sick. My body works to fight and kill the germs. This makes my body tired. I need to sleep.

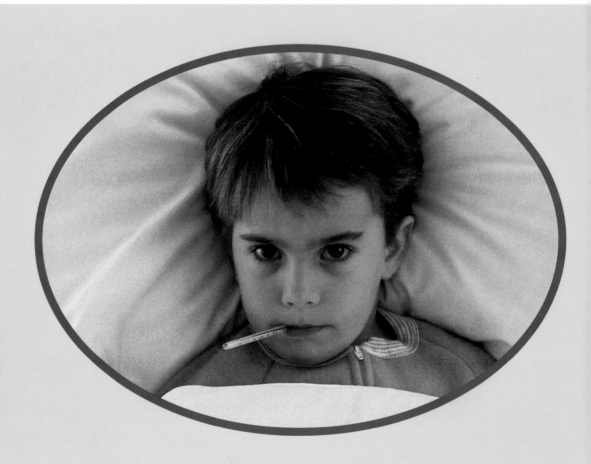

I stay home from school when I am sick.

If my body cannot kill the germs,
I go to the doctor. My doctor
looks at my body.

Sometimes I need
medicine to help
me get better.

How Else Do I Take Care of Myself?

I take care of myself in other ways, too. After working hard, I like to have fun. Sometimes I dance to music in my room.

My friends and I like to roller skate.

My family and I like to have fun together. We like to go for walks on the beach.

Having fun is a good way of taking care of my body.

Glossary

brush: to clean teeth with a toothbrush.

cavities: holes in teeth.

doctor: person who helps sick people.

exercise: movements to keep the body healthy.

floss: to clean between the teeth with string.

germs: tiny living things that can make people sick.

medicine: something to help a sick person get well.

Index